The Diary

by Catherine Burwell

Illustrated by Ann Johns

Chapter 1

You should see the inside of my school
blazer. It hasn't got soppy name labels
everywhere, or school badges. No. There
are six secret pockets. I sewed them on
myself. (Sounds unlikely, I know.) I keep
my important things in these pockets. And
why do I do that, you ask? Well, let's just
say that I move around a lot.

Anyway, I'll give you a quick guided tour inside, from left to right. First, my grandad's watch on a chain (not working). Next a bag of pound coins. I got them for washing people's cars. Then two Arsenal tickets from Wembley, 1992. It was an ace match. Everton got flattened. It was 3 – nil, to Arsenal. Next, there are

three photos of Steve (my brother) and my mum. Plus other important things: three packets of chewing gum, two torch batteries, and my bus pass. But last and most amazing of all is my diary. That is a grade one totally out-of-reach object. Which means NO ONE sees it except me. Not even you!

BZZZZZZZZZ!

That's the school bell. The first bell of the day, worst luck. Oh, and guess what? Here comes Crusher Crawford and his mates. Some people are scared of him. I'm not. I call him Crush a Crumb.

"What are you looking at?" he says to me.

"I don't know, but its looking back!"

I fly under his arm and run off
laughing. I hear him behind me. His feet
are tapping towards me down the
corridor. Quick, into the girls' loos. That'll
lose him. I'm half out of breath. Only
from surprise, mind you.

"Aargh! There's a boy in here!!"

"It's Figgy. Get out will you?"

"Get out!"

Girls can be so fussy.

"Oh, is this the ladies'?" I say, all
charm. "Well, I am sorry. Do get on with
your lipstick while I ..."

Crawford bursts through the door. In a flash, I've got a foot in the sink and I'm halfway out of the open window. Always a bit of a squeeze, this window. Oh! Something's caught on that stupid hook. I lean out. RIP! I fall to the grass below and

start running. Thirty metres or so away, I turn round. Crusher is nowhere to be seen. The screaming has died down too. He's probably being attacked by some Year Eleven girl who fancies him. I laugh aloud and make my way to the fire exit stairs.

Chapter 2

"Rebecca Damson?"

"Yes, Miss."

"Simon Fellows?"

"Yes, Miss."

"Joseph Figgins? Joseph Figgins? Joseph?"

The door swings open. "Yes, Miss?"

"Where have you been? You're late."

"Handing some extra homework in to Mrs Lewish."

"You mean Mrs Lewis?"

"Yes, except she talksh like thish."

The class bursts out laughing. Miss starts on at me about rudeness and speech problems. Better than detention problems, I always say. She's so busy with Mrs Lewis that she forgets to ask me any more questions. It works a treat. I should give lessons on it – dodging late detentions.

I settle down and pat my pocket for my diary. My diary... I look down at my blazer. There's a hole the size of a football.

I remember the hook, the rip. Oh no!
Oh no! Everything goes black. I feel sick. I
am imagining Crusher holding my diary.
Laughing. Reading things that weren't
meant for him to read. Pointing at the bits

about leaving Mum and Steve, and going to the kids' home. It's none of his flaming business. He'll be showing it to Cobber and Willis and the other idiots. He could be tearing out pages about me. About the things I need to keep ... to remember. I NEED that diary. It's ... it's ... ME!

Before I know it, I'm in front of Miss's desk.

"Miss, I think I've lost my pocket money."

She doesn't believe me.

"Go and sit down, Joseph. You've caused enough trouble for one morning."

"But Miss, it might be stolen if I leave it lying around. I'll have to go. I think I know where it is..."

I'm out of the door, racing down the stairway. Miss calls down the corridor.

"Joseph, Jo ... come back here... You'll be in ..."

"Detention." I finish the sentence for her. But I don't care about detention.

Denise + Scott

Jane ♡ Phil

I'm heading for the girls' loos, back along the polished floor. No one is in sight. Crusher and his lot are all in class, giving the teachers grief instead of me. Past the stock cupboard. With a sly look around, I dart into the girls' loos.

It's cool in here. I stand still and look.
Taps are dribbling. Bits of chewing gum
are all over the ceiling. My eyes settle on
the waste paper basket. Maybe?? I shake it
upside down. Oh, nothing! Just paper
towels and boxes of ... you know ... girls'
things.

I pull myself up to the window sill. I wonder if my diary has fallen outside? I peer over. There is nothing but grass. I drop back down. One foot in each sink, then on to the floor. The sick feeling comes back. I open my blazer to check it isn't a bad dream. It isn't.

Chapter 3

Thankfully, I bump into Stuart at break.
He is a real mate. We have known each
other ages. Two months, nearly.

"Stu – just the man!"

"Hey, Fig, got any stickers?"

"What?" I say. "Oh yeah, football stickers. No, I haven't. But listen, I need your help."

"Is it woman trouble, Fig?"

He's got a one-track mind, sometimes.

"No, of course it isn't woman trouble. I've lost something important. It's a book..."

I can't tell him it's my diary. It takes a while before people understand that sort of thing.

"A book, Fig? That's not like you."

"Yes, a book. I can read, you know. Look, just trust me. I think Crusher's got it."

"Ooh, nasty!"

"Come on, Stu. It's not that bad. All we need is a plan to get it back." I know that will get him interested.

We find a cosy spot under the coat racks and work it all out.

By lunch time everything is ready. Stu and me are eating dinner in the canteen. We have taken up positions at a side table. I can see the bag pile at one end of the room, and Stuart can see the dinner queue at the other end. The place is crawling with prefects, but the situation's under control.

After 10 minutes Crusher and Co. appear. They drop their bags off and join the dinner queue.

NOW! I leap to my feet.

"Excuse me, prefect, Stuart's feeling sick." I point to Stu who is dying nicely a few tables away.

The prefect leaves the pile of bags and goes over to see Stuart. I grab Crusher's bag and dive into the corridor.

I begin emptying it on the floor. There's so much junk in here that I shouldn't think he can find anything himself. It's like a black hole.

Suddenly, Crusher's right hand man,
Cobber, comes round the corner.

"Lost something?" he sneers.

"Nothing that you can help me find,
thanks very much," I reply.

He goes back into the canteen. That was close! Still, he is no threat to me without Crusher. I am throwing everything out and still no sign of my diary. It must be in here somewhere.

Before I get any further, Stuart comes tearing up to me.

"Crusher's coming after you!"

"But I haven't found it yet!"

"You'll have to put it back, Fig! You'll get done!"

"I can't stop now!" I scream, searching madly through the bag.

"Fig! He'll kill you!"

Stuart starts stuffing everything back in. I get the message.

"Stand on it, Stu. It won't close!"

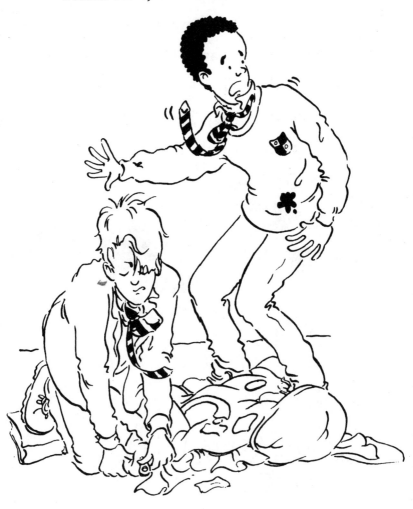

We zip up the bag and rush to fling it on the bag pile. We scrabble to find our own bags and run into Crusher at the door. I eyeball him for a micro-second. Then I see our escape. The dinner queue. We barge through.

"Out of the way. He's going to throw up!" I cry. Stu is right behind me.

"Get him to the sick bay toilet!" cries Mr Howard, making way for us.

Crusher is not so lucky!

"And are you going to sick bay too, Crawford? I don't think it needs three of you. You just go and sit down."

Once outside, we speed towards the
CDT room. Then we stop running.

"We made it!" gasps Stu. He is bent
double.

"Yeah!" I grin, out of breath. My face
changes. "But no blasted ... book."

"Maybe Crusher's got it on him?"
offers Stu.

"If he has, I've had it."

"And if he hasn't?"

"It'll be torn to shreds by now."

There is a short pause.

"You know what, Fig? I think you're having a bad day."

Chapter 4

All afternoon I am thinking about Crusher
finding out all my private things. Things
you would hardly even tell your best
friend. And now Crawford, of all people,
knows. I want to die.

It is five past three. I drag my coat along the dusty yard. I hear footsteps behind me. It'll be Carpy Parky, my form tutor, wanting me in detention. Or Crusher blinking Crawford throwing my secrets at me. Things don't get worse than this.

"Is this yours?"

The voice is quiet. It isn't Crawford. It's a girl. I swivel round. It is as though I am dreaming. I see my diary held out in a

girl's soft-skinned hand. My diary. My diary. Maybe Crawford has no idea. He probably hasn't even seen it. Let alone read it. My heart sings. I am delighted.

Suddenly all the terror of this morning comes back. The blood drains from my face. She is not Crawford. But she is someone I don't know. And she has read all about me. My diary has become a weapon and she is going to strike me with it.

"Well, is it yours? I saw you in the
toilets jumping out of the window and I
thought you dropped it."

I am speechless.

"What's the matter? I didn't even look
inside to check the name. Maybe it's no
big deal."

I repeat the words in my head. "I didn't even look inside..." It hits me like a blast of cold wind. SHE DIDN'T EVEN LOOK INSIDE!

"You mean you didn't read it? You didn't open it at all?" I blurt out like a prize wally.

"I just said that." (She is thinking what a prize wally I am.) "Do you want it or what?"

Try to be calm, Fig.

"Oh, yeah – I must've dropped it.
Thanks very much." I take my diary back.
It feels like velvet.

"Yeah, thanks very much," I continue.
I am about to walk away but she is
looking down. "Thanks – thanks for
bringing it to me." My diary. My diary.

"I wondered if it was important. I
looked all over the yard at lunch time for
you. But you weren't there. I don't know
who you are. I thought maybe I wouldn't
see you to give it back," she says.

"Yes, its lucky you found me," I say. "And kind of you to try."

She has a nice face. Sort of soft. Like my mother's was.

"Maybe see you tomorrow," I say. I am smiling.

She looks puzzled. Of course, she wouldn't know how to find me again.

"I'm in 9A," I explain.

"Oh, I'm in 8L – Mrs Lewis's class."

"Ah – Mrs Lewish."

We both laugh. I wonder whether tomorrow I might show her my Wembley tickets. Well, maybe just one. To begin with.